You Deserve This, Not That

You Deserve This, Not That

Living an Abundant Life after Near Death, Abuse, and Addiction

DEBORAH BRUNNER

Motivating the Masses, Inc.

CARLSBAD, CA

Editing and interior design: Tanya Brockett, www.HallagenInk.com

To my dear friend Patti:
Although you are no longer here among us on earth,
your loving spirit has guided me every step
of the way.

Sometimes you have to be willing to let go of something old to grab onto something new. You have to be willing to let a part of you die that you used to be comfortable with in order for another part of you to be born.

–LISA NICHOLS

CONTENTS

Acknowledgements

This book is dedicated to all the incredible, wonderful women of this world—the ones who shared their voice and their vision with us all. I was fortunate to meet some of these strong women throughout my life's journey; others I have yet to meet. I want to thank all of you for your powerful message of inspiration and empowerment. These women helped me to see and believe that I mattered in this crazy world.

Also, a special thanks to those friends and family nearest and dearest to me: Clara, Nicci, Mandy, Katie, Sandy, my parents—Red and Rosie, my sons—Michael and Trevor, my brother Mark, and my dear husband Corey. Thank you for always loving and supporting me during this adventure.

The Attack

"Why did this have to happen to me?"

"I don't want to die!" I cried, trying to steady my small, five-foot, frail body against the ice-cold vanity.

It was damp and chilly, just like the dreary April day outside. I tried to move, but my feet felt like they were chained to the brown shag carpet. My gaze darted around the tiny bathroom. I saw the golden colored toilet sitting perfectly under the stairs with its matching tub alongside. I could barely hear the soft laughter of my son, Michael, coming from the living room.

As I stared out past the bathroom and into the kitchen, my eyes began to blink uncontrollably. I couldn't believe what I was seeing! Somehow, like I had X-ray vision, I could see Donna through the thick, five-inch plaster wall that separated me from her.

A wave of panic quickly spread across my clammy, sweaty body, "What the hell is happening to me?"

I cried out, pleading, "Please help me, Donna! Please, please! I don't want to die!"

But Donna didn't move. She stood motionless leaning on the laminate kitchen counter.

I tried to call out again, but no sound escaped from my lips. My pleas were trapped deep inside my mind. Tears were pooling in my golden brown eyes. I felt absolutely helpless.

Suddenly, my neck jerked awkwardly to the left and my arms bent in front of me as if to protect me from a boxer's punch. My head snapped up towards the ceiling, and the bright, glaring light above the tub held my gaze like a deer caught in headlights. I was terrified!

My body was overcome with violent convulsions, jerking and thrashing around like a tiny rag doll. My head and back banged brutally against the wooden cabinet of the vanity. Then my body stopped. Stillness. My eyes gently closed. I knew death was there to claim me.

I remember *that* day like it was yesterday. It was the absolute best day of my life, and also the absolute worst. The best, because I LIVED. The worst, because I had suffered a heart attack. It was exactly sixteen days before my twenty-fifth birthday. That day was the biggest turning point of my life.

The days before my heart attack were dark and lonely with every minute consumed by drugs, deception, and despair. Nearly every decision I made was one of destruction, and everything surrounding me seemed the same.

I was living a life filled with lies. I lied. The people around me lied. No truth was to be found anywhere. Cheating, abuse, and addiction were a daily part of how I lived; they had moved in and become part of the daily grind. Over time, their roots had sunk so deep into my subconscious that it had become normal.

It's only recently that some of those terrible, daily occurrences have come back to the surface of my memory. They were buried so deep and for so long that even now, when I recall and talk about some of the memories with someone like you, I almost feel like I'm recounting a stranger's life. The life of a woman who had endured the beatings and the crushing torment of mental abuse.

Was it really me who had been living that life? Living with a man who was a wolf in sheep's clothing, who led me to believe that I deserved that kind of life, and who used words like "love" to disguise the rage he unleashed upon me? Yes, it was me; I was the one living with someone who didn't really love me the way anyone should be loved.

You see, I know what it's like to be that person who maybe didn't deserve a better life. At least it surely didn't feel like I deserved it. That's how I felt day after day for over seven years.

Still, throughout all the turmoil, even in the midst of it, I was deserving. The only person who couldn't see how truly special, how wonderful, and how deserving I was, was me.

Many times after my heart attack I found myself asking God, "Why? Why did this have to happen to me? Why didn't you just let me die?"

Still, throughout all the turmoil,
even in the midst of it, I was deserving.

I knew in my soul the answer was for me to be there for my son, Michael; he deserved a better life. I also knew another reason.

Ironically, the house in which I had the heart attack had once been a nunnery. I believe that all the prayers that they had offered up in that house somehow helped keep me alive.

Deep down, I yearned to give my son and myself a better life, and I knew that the only way that would happen was if I changed. I needed to start making better decisions and finally get my shit together. Rehab seemed like the perfect place to start.

Rehabilitation

No more blaming everyone else for my problems.

I was admitted into a rehabilitation program. I was only allowed to stay in treatment for ten days because I was on welfare at the time, and that is all that the state would cover. I was fortunate that my parents, Red and Rosie, watched Michael while I was admitted.

Now I wish I could tell you that from the moment I was released from rehab I was a changed person, that life was easy-peasy, and that I never struggled again. I wish I could proclaim how I immediately felt completely worthy, deserving, and lived as such the rest of my life. Wouldn't that be a great story? But the truth of it is, "hard" doesn't even begin to describe my journey out of *that mess.*

Over the years I had allowed that mess of a life to cultivate up around me, and the first step out of it was realizing that I had to be the one to clean it up, step by grueling step. No more blaming everyone else for my problems. The solution was *within* me—it *was me* the whole time.

The decisions that followed, which began clearing the path to a better life, were not easy. Yours will not be easy either. You may have to leave friends and maybe even family behind. You will turn from the familiar and comfortable things, the things that you believe are the source of your safety and security, and instead, you will have to walk into the open arms of the unknown.

You must if you want to survive.

THREE

I Need to Get Out

I desperately wanted a way out, a better life,
but I didn't know where to start.

I remember one evening, years before the attack, when I was in cosmetology school. I had gone out for dinner and drinks with my ex-husband's stepsister, Kim. We got home super late, around two-thirty in the morning. As soon as we walked in the door of our trailer home we saw how furious he was.

He immediately grabbed Kim by the hair and dragged her down the narrow hallway. He started hitting and punching her repeatedly! I yelled at him and begged him to stop, but he continued. I then began yelling and slapping him, pleading with him to let her go. He did. But then he turned the violence on me.

After being pummeled over and over again by his clenched fist, the world grew black and I eventually lost consciousness.

You would think I would remember such a horrific, unrelenting beating, but I don't. Years later as I began writing this book, Kim retold the details of that horrible night to me. While they were seared in her memory, I had not only forgotten that night, but also the fact that I had to miss several weeks of school because of the bruises and swelling over my entire body.

A few weeks after this incident I moved in with a friend from cosmetology school. Early one morning I went down to the Social Services department near her home. I sat on the sidewalk waiting eagerly for them to open. When they did, I was the first one in.

I walked over and began talking to the woman behind the desk. I explained my situation to her and stated that I needed to apply for assistance so I could leave my ex. She stared at me from behind the desk for a moment. Then she informed me that there was nothing they could do for me.

When I asked her why she explained that because I didn't have a permanent address, there was nothing she could do. I walked out the doors and sobbed.

So what do you think I did?

Yes, you're right; I went back to the abuse, the drugs, and the lies. After all, I was that stupid, ugly, idiotic girl that no one would help, right? My self-worth plummeted to an all-time low.

The only thing that helped take away the pain during that time was the drugs. I became so heavily addicted that I even began selling them. People were actually coming to our house at two o'clock in the morning, banging on the door, wanting to buy drugs from us.

I remember one time; I feared I was going to jail because six police cars had surrounded our house. I quickly hid everything as fast as I could. I was happy the baby was sleeping. Luckily for me, the police were at the wrong house. They were looking for someone on the other side of town so they never came in. Imagine what would have happened if they had.

I desperately wanted a way out, a better life, but I didn't know where to start. Maybe you find yourself struggling with this too. You've made the decision, but in the back of your mind, you're not sure how or where to begin.

FOUR

I Found How to Really Get Away

I had finally had enough of that life!

It wasn't until my ex-husband's brother accidently burned our son that I finally made the decision to leave my ex and move back to Wisconsin.

I remember being at the hospital with our little guy. When the doctor came into the room to ask what had happened, my ex said, "She did it," making it sound like I had intentionally hurt my son.

I'll never forget the piercing glare from the doctor, or the pain I felt from my ex's words. But it was just what I needed. Those words stung deeper than any punch he had ever given me. There was no way I was going to let this man, or anyone, ever say

I hurt my baby! I had finally had enough of *that* life!

I'm not going to tell you the journey into *this* new life is going to be easy—you will have to fight for it. But I can share with you that the challenging new situations you will go through are temporary. And even though they may seem like they will never end, let me assure you they will.

The beautiful, strong woman or man that you are will soon begin to emerge. Your courage and your strength will come through as you take each and every step forward. These stepping-stones will lead you to a place of personal growth and transformation. In *this* new abundant life, you're going to find joy, happiness, and become the person

You do deserve so much better than that.
You are worthy of a better life.

you were always meant to be. You may not be able to imagine it now, just how beautiful your life will be; but with all the hard work you're going to put into it, your life is going to be amazing!

I can tell you, it's here. It's yours. It's waiting for you.

Maybe you're terrified that as you begin the transition into *this* new life that you'll lose yourself.

I want you to understand that all you've been through will never be erased like chalk off a chalkboard. *That* life, *that* you, will become an amazing and integral part of you. The experiences you went through will empower you and give you strength in ways you can't even imagine.

You do deserve so much better than *that*. You are worthy of a better life. Now it's time to move on to *this* life. You don't have the choice to change the past. What has happened has happened. There is no changing the things we've done and the things that have been done to us. We can begin to understand that life is life and it isn't always fair. We can only control our choices and our actions. With this power of choice, we can make the decision to move forward and live in a different place.

FIVE

The Relapse and Rebound

Now when I look back, I don't even recognize myself. I feel the joy inside of me for the life that I now get to live.

After I had made the initial decision to move back to Wisconsin, I was delighted that I had stayed off the drugs. Sadly, I still didn't believe that I deserved a better life. So when I started dating someone who reintroduced me to cocaine, my life began to quickly spiral out of control.

Even though I wanted a different life, I hadn't really focused on creating a better life for my son and me. Consequently, within a few weeks I was living *that* life again and that's what led me to having a cocaine-induced heart attack at the young age of twenty-four.

Of course, the transition from addiction and abuse to abundance was met with many obstacles. I remember the inner need I had to prove to myself that I wasn't "stupid" and "dumb" like my ex had alleged for so many years. So I decided to attend a local Tech school.

I was so excited about this brand new opportunity. Unfortunately, the school I hoped to attend informed me that I had failed the reading comprehension test and would not be accepted for admission. I was so crushed and devastated. I immediately began to think my ex was right. Maybe I was that ugly, stupid, idiotic girl.

A few weeks later a friend of mine suggested I talk to the local community college. After speaking with the guidance counselor, I was shocked. He informed me that not only could I attend, but they would also help set up tutoring for me as well. This was another enormous turning point in my life! It gave me a huge confidence boost I desperately needed.

While I was a student, I even made the honor roll and the dean's list. This was the creation of a new spark, one of a true conscious belief that I *could* have a better life, and *maybe* even deserved it.

As a single parent, I found strength I never knew I had. I worked three jobs to put myself through college and I began to have dreams, goals, and ambitions again. Everyday my life became a little more joyous because I saw that I could overcome the challenges in my life and succeed. I began to be happy again and believed that I really could make things happen, and that life could be better; that even when I stumbled and fell, I'd get back up again.

I met so many incredible people while attending college. Some of them, like my friend Nicci, were single parents just like me. We knew that we were doing what was best, not just for ourselves, but for our kids too. The support we received from the teachers, the faculty, and even the other students was incredible.

I was also fortunate because I had the backing of my parents. They have been my rock throughout this new journey of abundance. It was difficult for all of us at the beginning, but I had to be honest with them. I needed to share all of the horrible secrets of the things I had done in my past. It was scary to be vulnerable with them. I was afraid they would reject me, and not want anything to do with their druggie daughter.

But the truth is, we became closer than I ever imagined we could. We all need people in our lives to be our support and to give us strength. I am blessed and honored they were able to do this for me.

All of these new experiences helped me to cultivate a new belief system. The old negative thoughts that once controlled me, seeing myself as nobody, someone who could never be loved, were being replaced. New, strong, incredibly confident ones emerged and with each triumphant step forward, I began to have a better life.

Now when I look back, I don't even recognize myself. I feel the joy inside of me for the life that I now get to live. Joy has become so much a part of my day-to-day life that I don't think I even fully realized it.

It was only six months ago when I was talking to one of my fellow Toastmaster (a public speaking club) friends. She was helping me put together a speech when I suddenly began to wail, "Oh my gosh, I don't even recognize who I used to be." I had never given myself permission to look back at my past. Now here I am "stunned" at how far I have come from that previous life.

Back when I first got clean, I was afraid I was going to lose me: that funny, quirky girl. I believed that if I quit the drugs, I wouldn't be interesting, fun-loving, and care free. The crazy thing is, it took me almost twenty-nine years to be able to realize that I was standing at peace with all of that: the good, the bad, and the ugly of my past. My family would often tell me that I became too serious, and they were right. I wish I could go back over those twenty-nine years and let myself enjoy every one of those days.

Someone once told me that I would never be "happy" in life. The truth is, it took me years to embrace the good things that were happening in my life. But over time, I found myself being grateful for the incredible things that were taking place. I had a caring husband, Corey, another beautiful son, Trevor, and all the overflowing abundance of life.

A word of caution: please be aware of the new situations and surroundings you're putting yourself into as you begin your new journey. Do not let anyone steal your smile. Intentionally be aware so that you can be safe.

When I say this to my children, who are so far removed from that life I once lived, I can see them walking away, rolling their eyes, and under their breath saying, "Oh God, here she goes preaching again."

Maybe they're right, maybe I do preach too much. But I am delighted to say that their lives don't resemble the life I once lived. They know what safety, security, and self-worth all feel like.

You deserve this too.

Find the joy in the good things...

I do hope that in reading this and in taking these first steps you can see just how great life is going to be and embrace each moment. Find the joy in the good things, like a new marriage, a new child, or whatever happens in your life. Look in the mirror and say to yourself: "I'm worthy of what I'm pursuing. I'm okay. I do deserve *this* better life."

Now you may be saying to yourself, "But Deborah, you don't understand. You don't know the horrible things that I've done. You don't know how rough, how difficult, and how painful my life's been."

First, I want you to understand that I agree with you. I know in many ways I could never possibly understand all that you've been through. Yet, on the other hand, I have been there. I've lived it. And, as hard as it may be for you to imagine right now, you can have a better life.

Again, it's going to take a lot of hard work. It's not an overnight transition to abundance, but if you continue working on the small steps, your life will become better. You will begin to heal. I'm here to help you; don't be afraid to let me guide you through this new journey.

When I first started, I would have small successes, which I would celebrate in some way or another, but I would almost always self-sabotage. Many times I'd fall back into the past with my self-limiting beliefs. I had negative thoughts like, "I can't do this! What's wrong with me? Who do I think I am that I deserve a better life? A good life and good things aren't going to ever happen in my life." Throughout my journey I've run into many people along the way who have felt the same way.

SIX

Defeating "That Life"

Today I get to show up as a strong confident woman living in a place of abundance and happiness.

One of my closest friends in recovery told me one time that she was worried about me because I was starting to drink a little bit. She was concerned that I was going to slip and fall back into my old using ways.

I discussed it with my husband who said, "I have alcohol around the house all the time and you never touch it. I'd say it just really isn't an issue for you."

I thanked her for her concern and reminded her that she really needed to focus on her recovery. This was something I think she wasn't ready to hear because it was a couple of weeks before I heard from her again. And what she said to me shook me to my core.

She said, "I've really never felt like an addict because I only was addicted to smoking weed. So what I'm thinking of doing is trying some coke with my friends. Because then when I go to meetings I can really be an addict."

I knew from my own personal experience, from the first time I tried cocaine, that it only took one time and I was hooked. I pleaded with her on the phone and tried to convince her not to do it. I tried to tell her that using cocaine wouldn't make her any more of addict than she already was. I was so scared for her.

Sadly, she made the choice to use. She is still alive, but she hasn't come back. She is still stuck in the devastating, destructive life of addiction.

All of us are pros at sabotaging our lives. It took me years to stop this self-destructive behavior. It's easier to live in the familiar than it is to change. The unknown is scary. As we take these bold first steps of declaring that we do deserve a better life, we open ourselves up to the possibility of who we truly can become. We seek out personal growth and self-transformation. We find books, videos, whatever we can to help us along this new journey.

My first self-help audio tape was Tony Robbins, and the first book I read was *The 7 Habits of Highly Effective People: Powerful Lessons in Personal*

Change by Stephen R. Covey. Their inspirational messages of change motivated me to become a better person. I encourage you to find people like Tony, Stephen, Lisa Nichols, and Deepak Chopra, and begin to allow those kinds of materials to pour into you. That will help you to see your self-worth. As you open yourself up, you will see that you are worthy and that you do deserve a better life.

I wish that I could take away all of your pain…remember, your pain is only temporary.

You will begin to surround yourself with uplifting, positive individuals who believe in you and your success. You will connect with people who will stand with you and help encourage you with this new self-growth. Find those who will help you build a strong foundation for abundance. They will lift you up until you really can see and believe how strong and worthy you are. My friends Sandy, Nicci, Clara, and Patti helped do this for me.

I wish that I could take away all of your pain. If I had that capability, I would do it for you in an instant. But remember, your pain is only temporary; what's going on now will not last forever. Life will be, and is already getting, better. Your most heartbreaking of moments, your situations and circumstances, that which may now seem unbearable, will not only become bearable, but will be replaced with joy. The beautiful, wonderful light that is in you; that's what is permanent.

Today I get to show up as a strong confident woman living in a place of abundance and happiness. I am feeling blessed in a wonderful marriage with two beautiful children. I am the president of my Toastmaster's club, which is crazy because five years ago I was terrified to speak in public.

I have also held numerous positions in my life. My friends call me the "variety woman" because of all the exciting jobs I've had. I was a soldier in the Army, I worked at a nuclear power plant, and I drove semis, to name a few. I used to be upset about this because I felt that I was a Jane of all trades and a master of none. But my son, Trevor, he didn't see it that way. He told me how fortunate I was to have experienced so much in my life because many people only dream about having these types of experiences.

It's hard to believe that I used to be somebody who struggled every day with domestic violence and drug addiction. I used to be a person who defined herself as unworthy of love, happiness, and success. I didn't really have hope for tomorrow.

For so many years, I've wanted to write a book about my journey to share with you the good, the bad, and the ugly of my personal story. But, there was always something stopping me. Maybe it was shame and guilt. The kind you have from the unimaginable things you have in your past. Maybe it was a fear of sharing my secrets with the world. What I've learned from all of this is how to be patient and wait.

I had asked God for the clarity and direction. Back on February 8, 2007, I saw Lisa Nichols on *The Oprah Winfrey Show*. She was talking about *The Secret* and I remember how her message resonated with me. She was so real and authentic. She didn't hide her past or pretend to be someone she was not. And her confidence and convictions were something I desired.

She had inspired me so much that I wrote a three-page entry that day in my journal. I would have given anything to see her in person. That was the beginning of this new chapter of my life's journey.

During the years that followed, I kept myself busy with family and work. I continued reading self-help books, but I was still searching for what I was supposed to do with my life. Then in 2011, a dear friend of mine, Patti, passed away. We were not speaking at the time so I had a tremendous amount of guilt about that.

I cried a lot over the next few weeks. And then I began to feel very sick. I went to see the doctor and he told me that I needed to have an emergency hysterectomy. He thought I might have cancer. Luckily, the tests were benign.

Over the next few months as I recovered from the surgery, I found myself asking God once again for clarity and direction in my life. I was certain that I had a deeper calling in my life. I found myself reading even more about living a life of purpose.

I began watching a considerable amount of spiritual shows on Oprah's TV network *OWN*. One day, I had the sudden feeling that I should go on the Internet and visit Oprah's website. When I did, I saw that they were giving away tickets for her upcoming Lifeclass in New York City. So I entered, hoping I'd win.

Fast forward to spring 2012. I am in New York City because I was fortunate to win the tickets! It was the second of April, which happened to be the anniversary of when I had gotten clean, and I sat in the audience, watching Oprah talk to Deepak Chopra on stage. Oprah shared her own story of life's trials and triumphs, and connected with the audience—with me—in a way that reached the deepest, darkest corners of my heart and soul.

In that moment, my purpose rang through my mind as clear as a bell: I too was going to share my story with others. The way she connected with and shared her story with the audience made it clear for me. There was absolutely no doubt in my mind. I knew that people just like you needed to hear this story. I needed to get out there and speak about it, even though the mere thought of doing so was terrifying.

In May of 2017, I met Lisa Nichols in person. This is just one of the amazing signs that my life has come completely full circle. Now, I am on an incredible journey of abundance. Not only that, having written this book, I am living out my purpose.

I hope that I have shared with you, more than anything else, that you deserve a better life. I hereby call you to be brave and bold. I dare you to find the nearest mirror, look yourself in the eye, and challenge the negative belief that is ingrained in your mind that says, "Who do I think I am that I deserve a better life?" Say to it, and to yourself, "I am amazing. I am beautiful. I am loved. I am worthy! Yes, I deserve a better life! *This Life, Not That*."

*How wonderful life is when you finally believe
you are worthy.*

– DEBORAH BRUNNER

SEVEN

Connecting with Deborah

As you begin your continuous transformation in worthiness and abundance, I encourage you to join our Facebook group called, "You Deserve This, Not That." In this group, you will find others who may be dealing with similar situations as yours. It is a discussion group where you can find answers, encouragement, and guidance to the many new questions you may have.

I am honored to inspire and empower those seeking a better life. Please note, any future e-courses, webinars, live workshops, etc., may be posted to the Facebook group and will be subject to change.

Resources

Domestic Violence

The list that follows contains websites and numbers for those seeking help with domestic violence.

National Domestic Violence Hotline: 1-800-799-
SAFE (7233) | 1-800-787-3224 [TTY]
www.domesticshelters.org
www.ncadv.org
www.domesticviolence.org

Addiction

Here is a list of websites available for those seeking help with addiction.

www.addictioncenter.com
www.americanaddictioncenters.org/rehab-
guide/free
www.na.org
www.drugabuse.gov
www.aa.org

About the Author

After a near death experience, Deborah Brunner was deeply motivated to change her life. She traded in her life of domestic violence and substance abuse for an incredible fulfilling life. Deborah's story, at least parts of it, is all too familiar in modern society. Where her story differs from most is not her will to live, which is remarkable, but beyond this point to a place where she picked up the pieces, reconnected with family, gained a degree, and continues to flourish, putting tough life lessons into meaningful action. It is a story of triumph.

Deborah's natural ability to engage and inspire will benefit anyone seeking to adapt, overcome, and excel over adversity. Her motivating story and impassioned plea is that you too can rewrite your own narrative. Deborah will unveil her experiences using humor and a gentle touch while sharing insights and wisdom to make her talks truly inspirational.

Deborah believes we should assist and applaud the will to survive, take time to listen, and stand and cheer those who triumph in the face of insurmountable adversity.

Her main website is www.DeborahSpeaks.com

Follow Deborah:
Twitter: https://twitter.com/deborahspeaks2
Facebook: https://www.facebook.com/deborah.p.brunner
E-mail: Deborah@DeborahSpeaks.com